W0008509

CITY CYCLING
NEW YORK

Text by Matt Seaton
Illustrations by Wren McDonald

Rapha.

Thames & Hudson

Original concept created by
Andrew Edwards and Max Leonard

Thanks to Adam Mansky, chairman of the board of directors
of Transportation Alternatives; Andrew McGee of RCC
NYC; Derrick Lewis, formerly of Rapha US; and Mike
Spriggs of Gage+DeSoto for their help with neighbourhoods

First published in the United Kingdom in 2018 by
Thames & Hudson Ltd, 181A High Holborn, London WC1V 7QX

City Cycling New York © 2018 Thames & Hudson Ltd, London

Designed by Michael Lenz, Draught Associates

Illustrations by Wren McDonald

British Library Cataloguing-in-Publication Data
A catalogue record for this book is available from the British Library

ISBN 978-0-500-29309-6

Printed and bound in China by Everbest Printing Co. Ltd

To find out about all our publications, please visit
www.thamesandhudson.com. There you can subscribe
to our e-newsletter, browse or download our current catalogue,
and buy any titles that are in print.

CONTENTS

Front flaps

LOCATOR MAP / A DAY ON THE BIKE

Back flaps

INFORMATION / MAP KEY

HOW TO USE THIS GUIDE

This New York volume of the *City Cycling* series is designed to give you the confidence to explore the city by bike at your own pace. On the front flaps is a locator map of the whole city to help you orient yourself. Here, you will see five neighbourhoods to explore: Central Park (p. 10); Lower East Side and Soho (p. 16); Dumbo and Williamsburg (p. 22); Prospect Park and Red Hook (p. 28); and Washington Heights and Inwood (p. 34).

Each of these neighbourhoods is easily accessible by bike, and is full of cafés, bars, galleries, museums, shops and parks. All are mapped in detail, and our recommendations for places of interest and where to fuel up on coffee and cake, as well as where to find a WiFi connection, are marked. Take a pootle round on your bike and see what suits you.

If you fancy a set itinerary, turn to A Day On The Bike on the front flaps. It takes you on a relaxed 35-km (22-mile) route through some of the parts of New York we haven't featured in the neighbourhood sections, and visits some of the more touristy sights. Pick and choose the bits you fancy, go from back to front, and use the route as you wish.

A section on Racing and Training (p. 40) fills you in on some of New York's cycling heritage and provides ideas for longer rides if you want to explore the beautiful countryside around the city. Essential Bike Info (p. 44) discusses road etiquette and the ins and outs of using the cycle-hire scheme and public transportation. And lastly, Links and Addresses (p. 48) will give you the practical details you need to know.

NEW YORK: THE CYCLING CITY

New York ought to be a fantastic cycling city. It has all the makings. The land is mostly flat, and where it's not, the views are magnificent. The skyscraper scenery is spectacular. It can be cold in winter and steamy in summer, but for most of the year the climate's fine. The culture, the food, the nightlife, are second to none. But all of this does not reckon with one very important factor: New Yorkers.

The local public radio station, WNYC, still plays as its signoff a prewar recording generally attributed to the great New Deal-era mayor, Fiorello LaGuardia: 'This is New York, city of opportunity, where more than 8 million people live in peace and harmony, and enjoy the benefits of democracy.' City of opportunity? Check. More than 8 million people? Check. The benefits of democracy? Check. Peace and harmony? Not so much. Or as a native New Yorker might say: 'Meh.'

And nowhere will you encounter the fractious, chaotic, cranky side of New York more than in the street. Forget the orderliness and safety of your northern European cities or the visionary urbanism of Scandinavian planning: New York is a town made by generations of thrusting, jostling immigrants, all trying to get ahead. It is a city built by the raw, rampaging energy of a capitalist monster, red in tooth and claw, a daily demonstration of creative destruction. The fast-buck ethos extends to your cycling environment: New Yorkers are always in a hurry (ever heard of a 'New York minute'?), and if you're not with the programme, you're going to be in their way. So don't expect courtesy from drivers. Don't expect consideration from the food-cart guy, the pizza-delivery dude, the snoozing cop in his carelessly parked cruiser, the stinky sanitation-department truck in the bike lane, the tourist riding the wrong way. The first rule of bike club? There are no rules.

But here's the thing for cyclists: there is no quicker way to know the city than to ride its mean streets. I don't mean to find your way around – though for most of the city, the gridiron layout makes navigation easy – but to find your way in. Cycling New York is your shortcut to becoming a New Yorker. Think of your initiation to riding a bike here as a kind of hazing ritual: it's nasty and scary at first, but once you pass, you're made.

And then all the other New Yorks open up to you. Manhattan, 21 km (13 miles) long and a little over 3 km (2 miles) wide, is bounded by the sea and three rivers – and an unfinished bike path. Lower Manhattan still shows traces of the old New Amsterdam in the tangle of irregular streets that make up the Wall St financial district. Above that, the poetry of neighbourhoods piles up its stanzas – Soho, Lower East Side, Greenwich Village, Chelsea, Murray Hill, Midtown, Morningside – all the way to Harlem and Washington Heights at the northernmost tip of the island.

Most of Manhattan's great bridges have bike paths, and from those elevations you see the Big Apple in the round, always seeming to revolve around the iconic core of the Empire State Building on 34th St, still totemic despite all the taller towers built since. The bridges also carry you into the boroughs of Brooklyn, Queens and the Bronx, each a city-within-a-city, worthy of exploration in its own right. Many partisans now consider Brooklyn far superior to Manhattan: less pricey, more livable, less SoulCycle, more locavore.

New York cycling is growing: the new arrivals in tech and media riding fixies are unfazed by the fears that haunt older New Yorkers, who remember the crime-ridden city of the 1970s and '80s, when you wouldn't go into Central Park after dark – and still think of riding a bike as about as dangerous. The Citi Bike share system has made a huge impression on the city, and is gradually colonizing 'the boros'. Never underestimate the traffic-calming potential of several thousand low-skilled cyclists every day: the Fred is your friend.

NEIGHBOURHOODS

CENTRAL PARK

AN URBAN OASIS FOR CULTURE AND RECREATION

Central Park is the green jewel set in the heart of Manhattan's grit and glitter. Following designs by architects Frederick Law Olmsted and Calvert Vaux, construction began in the 1850s and involved extensive landscaping – once its 700 acres had been cleared of the shantytown dwellings and livestock holdings of the free blacks and Irish immigrants who had lived there for several decades: an early chapter in the eternal New York story of real-estate development.

The park has been through several cycles of decline and degradation, including a period during the Depression in the 1930s when homeless unemployed workers built a new shantytown in the then-drained reservoir in the centre of the park: a 'Hooverville', as these settlements were called, after President Herbert Hoover, who had presided over the crash in 1929 and was blamed for the economic downturn. The 1936 screwball comedy *My Man Godfrey*, starring Carole Lombard, involves a Hooverville hobo adopted by a Park Ave socialite as her butler.

Even the park's present prosperous, well-groomed state is relatively recent: the infamous case of the rape and near-murder of the Central Park jogger in 1989 came at a time when it was considered a no-go area after dark. These days, the worst that is likely to happen is a ticket from the park police if you ride on the paths.

A good place to start is **Columbus Circle ❶**, at the northern terminus of 8th Ave. Motor traffic is mostly banned from the park drive, the 9.5-km (6-mile) circular road that swoops around the park's inner circumference. It's one way, anti-clockwise, so initially the route runs roughly parallel to 59th St (also known as Central Park South, where it borders the park). The first landmark on your right is **Wollman Rink ❷**, a spectacular skating facility in the winter – if you don't mind the Trump branding, which, as so often, the former real-estate mogul managed to leave behind long after he ceased to run the venue.

Follow the road round as it heads north past **The Lake ❸**. As you climb the short hill known to local riders as **Cat's Paw ❹** (keep your eyes open for the bronze sculpture of a mountain lion ready to pounce from

a big granite rock on the left), the rear elevation of the **Metropolitan Museum of Art ❺** comes into view. You can dismount and exit on foot here, but that cuts short the full glory of the **Museum Mile ❻**, the stretch of 5th Ave that runs along the park's eastern side and is home to no less than eight superlative museums and galleries.

It's worth going past for a glimpse through **Engineer's Gate ❼** of Frank Lloyd Wright's extraordinary masterpiece of ferroconcrete in the food-mixer shape of the **Guggenheim Museum ❽**, and exit instead down a short drive to 102nd St to check out the **Museum of the City of New York ❾**. Ten blocks south is another less-visited gem, the **Jewish Museum ❿**, a monument to the fact that American culture would be unimaginable without the contribution of the nation's Jewish citizens. The café in the basement is now run by Russ & Daughters (see p. 16), legendary Lower East Side purveyors of bagels and smoked fish.

Next up, before you get back to the incomparable 'Met', is the private **Neue Galerie ⓫** in a gorgeous Beaux Arts mansion on the corner of 86th St. It specializes in German Modernist shows, but the price of entry is justified almost alone for a view of Gustav Klimt's extraordinary shimmering-gold portrait of Adele Bloch-Bauer.

If it's time to caffeinate and refuel, then highly recommended is **Bluestone Lane ⑫**, just below the Guggenheim. A favourite with park racers, it's easy to find – right next to the aptly named **Church of the Heavenly Rest ⑬**. And you're just two minutes from the Met. A crucial tip for the out-of-town visitor is that unless you're paying to see one of the ticketed special exhibitions, entry to the permanent collections need cost you only a dime. Despite prompts to the contrary, only a voluntary donation is suggested, so save your cash for the excellent shop.

For the more intrepid cyclist, the quickest way to get across the park is to share with motor traffic one of the transverse roads, cleverly concealed from park users by deep cuts. There's one at E 79th St, directly below the Met, which brings you out at the Museum of Natural History (see A Day On The Bike). You're now on Central Park West, home to numerous Modernist apartment buildings, from the twin-towered elegance of **The San Remo ⑭** to, higher up, **The Eldorado ⑮** – both favoured by generations of movie stars.

Heading back down towards Columbus Circle brings you to **The Dakota ⑯**, most famous as the residence of John Lennon and Yoko Ono, and outside which Lennon was killed in 1980. Nearby, inside the park, is **Strawberry Fields ⑰**, an area dedicated to his memory. Re-entering the park here brings you to the recently restored **Tavern on the Green ⑱**, opposite the finish line for the New York marathon (and some bike races). Originally built by Calvert Vaux to house the sheep that grazed on the park's southern meadow, the building now houses a restaurant, immortalized in the film *Ghostbusters*. It also does a pretty good brunch for a not-horrible price.

REFUELLING

FOOD	DRINK
Loeb Boathouse ⑲ for brunch with a view	**Caffè Storico ㉑**, for a good *birra* with your meal
Park West Cafe and Deli ⑳ is the classic eclectic New York City diner	**Met Roof Garden Cafe and Martini Bar ㉒** for cocktails above the park's forest canopy

WIFI

Check email at **Le Pain Quotidien ㉓** in the historic Mineral Springs pavilion above the Sheep Meadow

LOWER EAST SIDE & SOHO

NEW YORK'S NEW BOHEMIA

No tour of the Lower East Side – once a byword for slum-dwelling poverty, now the 'LES', hub of all that is hip in fashion, food and art – is complete without a visit to the **Tenement Museum ❶** on Orchard St, just below the east–west thoroughfare of Delancey St. The museum's guided tours of its unlit, cramped immigrant housing is a brilliant physical record of the privations suffered by refugees and migrants from Italy, Russia and Eastern Europe in the late 19th and early 20th centuries. Call it the dark side of a visit to Ellis Island and the Statue of Liberty.

For a taste of the Jewish cuisine of the old LES, visit the new café run by **Russ & Daughters ❷**, also on Orchard. For more than a century, the firm's shop a block up on E Houston St has sold smoked fish: all kinds of lox (smoked salmon), as well as sturgeon and sable. Enjoy the same at the café, with bagels, bialys, blinis and blintzes, with dill and sour cream. Just around the corner is the **Mercury Lounge ❸**, one of New York's premier indie music venues. (Note that the street is pronounced *how*-ston, unlike the city in Texas, which is pronounced *hue*-ston: if you get it wrong, then 'Houston, we have a problem.') The Mercury is the smaller, try-out venue of the nearby, larger home of alternative rock, the Bowery Ballroom, under the same management.

Head east on Delancey and turn right onto the Bowery. Long known as New York's 'skid row', the Bowery was notorious for the 'bums' who frequented its cheap bars and flophouses. No. 315 was home for nearly 30 years to the club **CBGB ❹**. Originally intended as a venue for country, bluegrass and blues (hence the name), it became almost accidentally the capital of the New York punk scene, where acts like Television, Patti Smith, Blondie, the B-52s, Talking Heads and the Ramones first made their mark. It's now a Patagonia clothing store, which is perhaps a suitable metaphor for the retail-led gentrification of the area.

On the Bowery, opposite the eastern terminus of Prince St, our key corridor for this excursion, is the sleek, gleaming façade of the **New Museum ❺**, dedicated to showing contemporary art by living artists. If the art has left you thirsty, stay on the Bowery, take a left on Houston, and on the north side, at Elizabeth St, is **Tom and Jerry's ❻**, a neighbourhood joint where they serve a generous Negroni and you can still hear yourself speak at cocktail hour. Alternatively, double back on Rivington and keep your eyes peeled for Freeman Alley, at the end of which is **Freemans Restaurant ❼**, a great 'secret' place for contemporary American fare and cocktails. But if you just thirst for a good beer on a warm summer night, then virtually opposite is the tented yard of **Loreley Beer Garden ❽**.

Next, aim for Prince St, heading west. You are now entering Soho, or SoHo, to denote its original derivation from 'South of Houston'. Most of the district's buildings date from the mid-19th century, and the key features to note are the cast-iron columns. These pillars, which created Soho's famous airy loft spaces, represented the summit of building technology in the era before steel erection and elevators made highrise buildings possible at the dawn of the 20th century.

Check out the side streets paved with 'Belgian blocks', or, as we cyclists prefer to call them, 'pavés'. Now landmarked as the cast-iron district, much of Soho would have been levelled in the early 1960s to make way for Robert Moses's Lower Manhattan Expressway if not for Jane Jacobs, the legendary West Village community activist and urbanist. The fight back, led by Jacobs, saved the area, including Washington Square Park – beloved for decades by folk singers, protesters and NYU students.

Stay on Prince past **St Patrick's Old Cathedral ❾**, historic home to Catholic New York, and **McNally Jackson ❿**, one the city's few remaining independent bookstores. When you cross Lafayette, on your left is **Bicycle Habitat ⓫**, a solid city bike store with full workshop and repair service. You're now in the heart of Soho's shopping district – although, really, all of Soho could be described that way. Cut a block south down cobbled Crosby St to Prince St's parallel, Spring St, for the **MoMA Design Store ⓬** and for a smart lunch venue, **Balthazar ⓭**, and next-door coffee shop and bakery.

You'll want to hurry across the crowds of tourists on Broadway, but its intersection with Prince St is still the location of the original **Dean & DeLuca ⓮**, the pioneering posh deli when some of the lofts in Soho still had artists living in them, rather than providing office space for fashion app tech startups. The upside, perhaps, is that there's now an **Apple Store ⓯**, if you need one, at the Greene St intersection.

West of Broadway, Soho calms down a bit and you'll still find the odd hold-out art gallery in the surrounding streets, though most of the gallerists have long since fled to cheaper digs in Chelsea. High-end fashion has moved in behind the art: Marc Jacobs, Diane Von Furstenberg, DKNY, Armani and a horde of others vie for your dollars. On the block over from the north–south street called West Broadway is our old friend the Rapha Clubhouse (see A Day On The Bike). But if you fancy a takeout sandwich, then right opposite is the picturesque old-timey frontage of the **Vesuvio Bakery** ⓰. You could take that sandwich, along with a coffee from next-door **La Colombe** ⓱, to the mini-park down Thompson St. If you're with young kids, they will love a splashabout in the wading pool at **Vesuvio Playground** ⓲.

As Prince St runs into the bottom of 6th Ave, it becomes Charlton St. On that next block is the **Greene Space** ⓳, worth checking out as the performance space for live music and broadcasts for New York's public radio stations: WNYC and its classical-music sister WQXR, both housed in the building. One block down on Varick St is the **City Winery** ⓴, a great venue for those too old for the mosh-pit experience of the Mercury Lounge: a small stage with great sound, and cabaret club-style tables with great wine and a good menu. Stay west on Spring St to almost the last block, before you hit the West Side Highway, and get a nightcap at the historic **Ear Inn** ㉑. Billed as New York's oldest bar, this joint has served drinks for a century before the Prohibition era and many decades since, and is now also a live-music venue, three nights a week.

REFUELLING

FOOD
La Gamelle ㉒ for surf 'n' turf, Belgian-style
Hampton Chutney Co. ㉓ offers a modern
American take on Indian *dosa* cuisine

DRINK
Gimme! Coffee ㉔ brews up Fair Trade's
finest on Mott St
Soho Room ㉕ for mojitos and so much more

WIFI
Housing Works Bookstore Cafe ㉖ makes you feel smarter just being there

DUMBO & WILLIAMSBURG

HIPSTER CENTRAL FOR MUSIC, BARS AND GOOD EATS

New York is such a city of bridges and tunnels that there's even a Manhattanite term for the poor benighted people who live in the suburbs, especially New Jersey: the bridge-and-tunnel crowd. Somehow, Brooklyn escapes the scope of this snobbery – not least because Brooklyn has become, in many ways, a hipper alternative 'capital' of New York to Manhattan, a shift in cultural power reflected in the election of Park Slope resident Bill de Blasio as mayor of the city in 2014.

Tunnels are fine for subway riders, but bridges are great for cyclists. For this excursion, we're going out via the **Manhattan Bridge ❶**, rather than the Brooklyn Bridge, because the latter – though older, more historic and charismatic – has a narrow bike path that's filled with tourists virtually 24 hours a day. From on-ramp to off, the Manhattan Bridge soars up for over a mile across the East River from the lower end of Chinatown on the Manhattan side and deposits you near the Brooklyn waterfront.

Reaching Dumbo is easy: once at street level, just follow the line of the bridge back to the water. Dumbo gets is name from 'Down Under the Manhattan Bridge Overpass' – though the comedian Jerry Seinfeld once joked that the 'O' for Overpass was added solely to save the locals from living in a place called Dumb. Like Soho, the area once dominated by commerce and light industry was first regenerated by artists looking for cheap studio space in its warehouse lofts, and now commands some of the highest rents in the borough.

If you visit on a Sunday, you can check out the stalls and street food of **Brooklyn Flea ❷** in Pearl Plaza, a cathedral-like public space formed by the stone arch of the bridge's Brooklyn footing. By following the bridge's shadow, you'll emerge at the top end of the new, elaborately landscaped Brooklyn Bridge Park. But take a left under the bridge and along Water St and you pass **Atrium Dumbo ❸**, which offers a modern American take on French cuisine. Nearby, you'll find the historic Tobacco Warehouse, now home to **St Ann's Warehouse ❹**, perhaps New York's premier off-Broadway venue for theatre and live music. If you fancy a 'slice of pie', duck under the Brooklyn Bridge (see p. 28) for **Grimaldi's ❺**, one of the oldest and best pizzerias in New York.

Thus fortified, turn around and head back under the Manhattan Bridge, down Front St, until it brings you out at Navy St. This marks the southern edge of the **Brooklyn Navy Yard** ❻, a shipbuilding dock since the days of the American Revolution and a military installation from 1801 to 1966. The battleship *Missouri*, which received the Japanese surrender in 1945, was built here. Head east on Flushing Ave, an unpretty industrial thoroughfare that is the most efficient route until it crosses Bedford Ave, where you take a left and head north. You're now in the heartland of Brooklyn's Hasidic Jewish community. Large families are the norm here, and you'll probably notice the preponderance of people-carriers parked in the sidestreets.

Follow Bedford all the way under the on-ramp of the **Williamsburg Bridge** ❼ into hipster central: go-to destination for vintage clothing and vinyl record stores, artisanal jewelry and coffee shops, bars, clubs and no end of cool hangouts. Head towards the waterfront if it's a Saturday for the street-food spectacular of **Smorgasburg** ❽ in the East River State Park, where you can sample the wares of many of Brooklyn's notable restaurants. If it's later in the day and you've ever found yourself craving a cocktail and a savoury snack to enjoy while watching a movie, then the **Nitehawk Cinema** ❾ on N 1st St is made for you – with waiter service at your seat.

A few blocks down Metropolitan Ave from Bedford is the **Knitting Factory** ❿, initially a tiny avant-garde venue featuring musicians like John Zorn and Bill Frisell, which has grown into an indie-music powerhouse of record label, gastropub and festival and event organization. Bang opposite is Williamsburg's quirky answer to Manhattan's august city-history museums, **City Reliquary** ⓫, a community nonprofit that displays an eclectic collection of artefacts and historic bric-a-brac. It might be the only place you'll see an old subway token.

On a hot summer day, no visit to Williamsburg is complete without an ice cream. There are no bad choices, but recommended is the neighbourhoody joint **Azucar** ⓬ on S 4th St for its Latin-inspired flavours, including Dulce de Leche (caramel) and El Mani Loco (crazy peanut). The sugar high will help carry you up the long ramp of the Williamsburg Bridge. The views are great: first into people's apartments, and then, as you near the East River, over the red-brick behemoth of the old **Domino Sugar Refinery** ⓭, now being converted into upscale, molasses-infused apartments.

The views north of Manhattan as you come off the bridge are spectacular, with the regular blocks of the great postwar affordable housing development of Stuyvesant Town–Peter Cooper Village a notable landmark. You know you're back in Manhattan again when you hit ground on **Delancey St** ⑭, immortalized in the lyric of the old Rodgers and Hart song recorded most famously by Ella Fitzgerald: 'It's very fancy/ On old Delancey.'

REFUELLING

FOOD
Vinegar Hill House ⑮ serves up innovative contemporary American fare

Head to **Rye** ⑯ for hearty grub, speakeasy-style

DRINK
Brooklyn Roasting Company ⑰ for old-school aesthetics, thoroughly modern coffee

Lucky Dog ⑱ is the archetypal Bedford Ave saloon

WIFI
Bluestone Lane Dumbo ⑲, solid signal with all the accoutrements

PROSPECT PARK & RED HOOK

BROOKLYN'S WORTHY RIVAL TO CENTRAL PARK

A visit to New York can hardly be complete without a trip across the iconic **Brooklyn Bridge ❶**. The first steel-wire suspension bridge in the world, it was begun in 1869 and completed in 1883, and partly financed by renting out space under its Manhattan footings as wine cellars. It pays to make an early start, as the bridge gets very busy with foot traffic. As you roll down the long exit ramp off the bridge, note the unlovely landmark of the **Watchtower ❷** on your right, formerly the world headquarters of the Jehovah's Witness movement.

At Tillary St, take a left, continue for one block and then turn right into the new protected bike lane running along most of Jay St. Continue past the government centre of downtown Brooklyn, and follow the marked bike lanes by turning left, just before the Brooklyn Criminal Court, onto Schermerhorn St, named for a Dutch shipping family. Right onto Hoyt, then left onto Dean, into the heart of those bywords for gentrification, Boerum Hill and Park Slope.

Turn right onto 5th Ave, Park Slope's high street, which still retains some small artisan shops and restaurants. And then left, up St John's Place until it hits the bike lane along **Grand Army Plaza ❸**, with its triumphal arch dedicated to the Union soldiers and sailors of the Civil War. The southern end of the plaza now hosts a busy farmers' market on Saturdays, and leads to Prospect Park's inner ring road. The park's 5.3-km (3.3-mile) loop is largely closed to traffic and is used for bike and foot races, as well as recreational riders and runners of all stripes.

Near the Grand Army Plaza entrance to the park is the **Brooklyn Botanic Garden ❹** and the underrated **Brooklyn Museum ❺**, which has decent eating options with the **BKM Cafe and Bowl ❻**. Beyond beckons South Brooklyn and, at its terminus, the Atlantic Ocean. To see the sea, exit the park on the far side, at Machate Circle – near the Parade Grounds baseball fields where Sandy Koufax of the Brooklyn Dodgers learned to pitch. There, find the bike path that takes you along the 9-km (5.5-mile) **Ocean Parkway ❼** and follow it as it curves left and tracks the Prospect

Expressway. At Church Ave, cross Ocean Parkway and join the bike path on the far median, America's first dedicated bike path, built in 1894. Once on the bike path, you can ride Ocean Parkway all the way down to Coney Island for a stroll along the famous boardwalk (now made of cement, since Hurricane Sandy) or a ride on the wooden rollercoaster.

Rather than retracing your route from the bridge to the park, an alternative is to ride back through Carroll Gardens, via the old docklands of Red Hook, and along the waterfront to the Brooklyn Bridge. Take the Prospect Park West two-way bike lane, heading west to 2nd St. Cut down 2nd through Park Slope, until it dead-ends at 4th Ave; follow a quick left with a right onto 3rd St, which crosses the Gowanus Canal, known as the 'Lavender Lake' for its unnatural colour.

At Smith St, you're in Carroll Gardens, formerly a strongly working-class Italian neighbourhood. A right onto Smith followed by an immediate left onto 2nd Pl brings you to Court St, the local high street. The plain church on the left, **St Mary's Star of the Sea** ❽, was where Al Capone was married. The Italian restaurants **Frankies 457** ❾ and its sister **Prime Meats** ❿ both offer excellent dining.

Before crossing at Hamilton Ave, consider a pit stop at **Other Half Brewing Co. ⓫**, a tasting room and brewery tucked away on Centre St, for some of the best IPAs in America. (One of the founders, Sam Richardson, was a racer with the local Rapha team.) Head under the Brooklyn–Queens Expressway, and you're in Red Hook, a former port and the site of the union battles that inspired the film *On the Waterfront*. Once known as the 'crack capital of the country', today Red Hook has a hip, artsy vibe, and is home to the now-famous fixie bike race, the Red Hook Crit.

Proceed down Court to Bay St, and right along Red Hook Park, where at weekends you'll find **Red Hook Food Vendors ⓬**, whose trucks originally served local Latino soccer players. The Mexican *quezahuaraches* from **Country Boys ⓭** and Salvadoran *pupusas* from **El Olomega ⓮** are terrific. Off Bay St, make a left on Columbia St and follow the bike arrows right onto the bike path through **Erie Basin Park ⓯**, past the imposing, dystopic Red Hook Grain Terminal. Skirt the Ikea store at Beard St, turn left and rumble over the cobbles until you reach Van Brunt. If you take a left and pass the open gate, you'll end up on the Beard St Pier, with the best head-on view anywhere of the Statue of Liberty.

Finally, head to one of the neighbourhood's destination restaurants, such as **Hometown Bar-B-Que ⓰** (renowned for its brisket), **Brooklyn Crab ⓱** or **Lobster Pound ⓲**, followed by dessert at **Baked ⓳**. Or savour a cocktail at St John Frizell's **Fort Defiance ⓴**. Back to the bridge is easy: follow the bike lane on Conover and King St all the way to Columbia Terrace, make a left on Atlantic Ave and into Brooklyn Bridge Park. Follow the bike path to the end of the park, by the foot of the Brooklyn Bridge, where you'll find the **Brooklyn Ice Cream Factory ㉑**, worth a stop for a cone and a couple of scoops if the lines aren't too long.

REFUELLING

FOOD	DRINK
Scottadito ㉒ for traditional Tuscan cuisine	At **Red Hook Bait & Tackle ㉔** the Guinness
La Cigogne ㉓ for Alsatian specialties (no dogs)	is good – and so is the taxidermy

WIFI

5th and 7th Aves in Park Slope offer plenty of options for laptop-friendly signals:
Cafe Grumpy ㉕ (on 7th) and **Gorilla Coffee ㉖** (on 5th) work

HUDSON RIVER

EAST RIVER

BROADWAY

BROOKLYN BRIDGE

FURMAN ST

HICKS ST

BROOKLYN
HEIGHTS

COURT ST

COLUMBIA ST

CONGRESS ST

478

DEGRAW ST

278

23

CARROLL
GARDENS

18 DELEVAN ST

24

9

VAN BR ST

19

10

COLUMBIA ST

CLINTON ST

COURT ST

WEST 9TH ST

20

8

17

16

11

BEARD ST

SMITH ST

GOWANU

15

14 BAY ST

12

278

3RD AV

4TH AV

13

18TH ST

19TH ST

20TH ST

1 MILE = 4 MINS

1 KM

WASHINGTON HEIGHTS & INWOOD

A HIDDEN GEM OF HISTORIC MANHATTAN

If it wasn't for the George Washington Bridge (see A Day On The Bike), gateway to the Palisades and the Hudson Valley, few visiting cyclists would ever be likely to visit this end of Manhattan, which is a great shame as it contains many hidden gems of New York history, heritage and attractions.

The natural way to reach the bridge is to ride up the Hudson River Park bike path – actually reaching the bridge's walkways involves doubling back over a footbridge across the Henry Hudson Parkway, which flies under the bridge's Manhattan-side ramps. But it's easy enough to navigate to the W 176th St approach either via **Riverside Dr ❶** or by taking **St Nicholas Ave ❷** all the way up from Central Park; both routes make pleasant enough rides. But instead of crossing the bridge, follow Fort

Washington Ave north. A few blocks further on, **Bennett Park ❸** opens up on your left, opposite the 181st St subway stop. The park marks the site of Fort Washington, defended by the Continental Army against British troops in 1776, and, at almost 81 m (265 ft), the highest point in Manhattan.

At the northern end is the **Hebrew Tabernacle of Washington Heights ❹**, testament to decades before and after the Second World War when the neighbourhood was so popular with Jewish immigrants from Germany and Austria that it was known as Frankfurt-on-the-Hudson. Since the 1960s, it has become a predominantly Hispanic area, particularly popular with Dominican-Americans, drawn by the Heights' stock of solid, middle-class apartment buildings and relatively affordable rents.

If you're ready to re-up on caffeine, head another block up and drop in at **Cafe Buunni ❺**, a hip little coffee shop specializing in Ethiopian brews. From here, back onto Fort Washington Ave until it turns into Margaret Corbin Dr, named for a woman who took her wounded husband's place 'manning' the cannons in the defence of Fort Washington. She was also the first woman to receive a military pension, only 200 years before the US Army decided that women could serve in combat roles.

You're freewheeling now into **Fort Tryon Park ❻**, named for the last British governor of New York. It's a beautiful park sitting atop the ridge of Manhattan schist, with great views across the Hudson, but the chief attraction here is **The Cloisters ❼**. Like the park, the building was a gift from the Rockefeller family, and was constructed in the 1930s out of cannibalized parts from five French cloistered abbeys, dismantled and shipped stone by stone from Europe, and then reassembled by the architect Charles Collens, a Gothic Revival specialist. The Cloisters is part of the Metropolitan Museum of Art (see p. 11), which uses the space to display its collection of medieval art and artefacts. The **Trie Cafe ❽** makes a decent pit stop onsite here.

To ride out of Tryon Park, you have to retrace your route. Better is to go on foot the short distance down the steep eastern flank of the park and rejoin Broadway. Welcome to Inwood. Head north and you immediately hit Dyckman St, another reminder that New York was New Amsterdam before it was New York. If you're in need of a spare inner tube, turn left on Dyckman and the **Tread Bike Shop ❾** has you covered. Stay heading west and the street terminates at a boat marina with a restaurant of the same name, **La Marina ❿**, with a seafood menu and outdoor seating.

From this point the rest of Manhattan's northern tip is all park, **Inwood Hill Park ⓫**, a naturally landscaped gem of virgin forest that seems too good to be true for a neighbourhood that's still on the A-train. (If only biking was permitted on the trails … though your chances of running into a park ranger are admittedly slim.)

The northern end of the park is bounded by a narrow neck of water that connects the Hudson with the Harlem River and is known as **Spuyten Duyvil Creek ⓬**, literally 'spouting devil' in Dutch, because of the vicious tidal currents that swirl in this short estuary. The creek's course was altered in the early years of the 20th century to cut a channel for shipping, which resulted in the administrative oddity of the little neighbourhood of **Marble Hill ⓭** becoming geographically part of the Bronx, yet remaining for political purposes in the borough of Manhattan (hat tip for this curious fact to Eben Weiss, a resident of nearby Riverdale in the Bronx and better known as Bike Snob NYC).

If you want to explore the Bronx further, the Broadway Bridge carries you over the creek. Not much further north is **Van Cortlandt Park ⓮**, where cyclists can join the Old Putnam Trail, and from thence to the Old Croton Aqueduct Trail, the route of the remarkable early 19th-century brick tunnel that fed fresh water by gravity from some 64 km (40 miles) north into the city's central reservoirs. But that would be a whole other chapter …

Heading back down Broadway, Inwood's down-to-earth charms are apparent: Irish pubs, pizza places and tortilla joints. But look right at 204th St for one more landmark: the weird site of a stone and clapboard farmhouse on a garden plot. This is the **Dyckman Farmhouse ⓯**, a colonial-era holdout amid the apartment buildings, dating from about the 1780s. Its collection of old New York artefacts is open (albeit with limited hours) Thursday through Sunday.

Roll back down to Dyckman St and the choice of eats improves dramatically: a craft beer beckons at **The Park View ⓰**. For something with more of a kick, try **Papasito Mexican Grill and Agave Bar ⓱**, and for unfamiliar fusion cuisine, give the Japanese-Mexican mix at **Mamasushi ⓲** a go. Worth remembering, as you tuck in, is that the Dyckman St stop on the A-train is just across Broadway – and you can always take your bike on the New York subway.

REFUELLING

FOOD
Tryon Public House ⑲ has a draught list
that's impossible to fault

DRINK
Inwood Local ⑳ is neighbourhoody, with nachos
Le Chéile ㉑ for Irish brews and high spirits

WIFI
New York Public Libraries offer free WiFi in their
Fort Washington ㉒ and **Inwood** ㉓ branches

RACING & TRAINING

You may be collecting your pension before the Tour de France comes to New York, which is a shame because the city would make an incredible stage for a Grand Départ. It's not a totally implausible scenario, because New York will close roads for big NYC-branded sports events like the marathon, the triathlon and the Gran Fondo. But the prestige and popularity of cycle sport in the US took a big hit in the wake of the Lance Armstrong debacle, and the political will isn't there yet.

At grassroots, things look better. There is a thriving racing scene, thanks to spring and summer race series in Central Park (see p. 10) and Prospect Park (see p. 28) in Brooklyn. You need to be an early bird, though: races in both parks generally take place between about 6 and 8am, or even earlier as daylight permits. Races in Central Park are run under the auspices of the **Century Road Club Association**, founded in 1898 and one of the oldest and largest cycling clubs in America. Only CRCA-affiliated clubs are eligible for most races (the **Rapha Cycling Club** is one). For racing dates in Prospect Park, consult **BikeReg**, the go-to resource for all US racing calendar events, including fondos and sportifs.

On any morning, the park road is busy with training riders, most of the year round. Generally, you can jump in a group and take a turn, but if it's team-led, it's best to ask permission to join. Be aware that after 8am, parts of the roadway may be opened to car traffic, and traffic signals may be enforced by park police. Before that, cyclists can generally go at training pace without pause, but it is up to all riders to use the road with care and consideration towards runners, dog walkers, muggers and vagrants.

At weekends, for most New York City cyclists, there is essentially one exit from the city. This is to ride up to Washington Heights, past the Upper West Side, and cross the Hudson River over the George Washington Bridge (or the GWB, as it is commonly called). The view from the massive, 80-year-old suspension bridge linking Manhattan to the glacier-carved cliffs of the Palisades on the New Jersey side is truly one of the wonders of the world. On most days, you can see all the way down to Staten Island and the Statue of Liberty, some 24 km (15 miles) away. And if you stop in the middle of the bridge to take it in, you'll also feel the bounce of the thousands of tons of riveted, bolted steel beams under your feet as the tractor-trailer trucks rumble by behind you.

Not for nothing is the GWB where the hugely popular **Gran Fondo** starts. Once on the Jersey side, you're more or less obliged to ride north up the Hudson Valley, but you have a choice of using the 9W, a two-lane highway, or dropping down and looping back under the bridge to ride northwards on River Rd, cut into the Palisades for about 11 km (7 miles), out to a district called Alpine. It's not exactly alpine, but there is a good climb to finish, which takes you back onto the 9W.

Important to know is that on rural roads where the highway has a broad shoulder, cyclists are expected to use it, rather than the main lane. Towns may also have local ordinances calling for cyclists to ride in line, not abreast. In Piermont, for example, 32 km (20 miles) up the valley, which gets a lot of weekend cyclist traffic, the cops are trigger-happy with their ticketing. In a city the size of NYC, it can seem weirdly restrictive to have only one main route out of town, but it also creates an automatic community of weekend riders. If you get as far as the nearby Hudson Valley towns, don't miss the cafés: **Bunbury's** in Piermont and, in Nyack, the **Runcible Spoon Bakery** and the **Gypsy Donut and Espresso Bar**.

For a serious endurance ride, stay on 9W all the way out to Harriman State Park and take Perkins Memorial Dr up to the park's highest peak of Bear Mountain. It's a 161-km (100-mile) round trip, but you can cheat by crossing the river near Bear Mountain and catching a Metro-North train home from Peekskill on the east side of the Hudson. While you're riding around Harriman, keep a lookout for all the fine stonework of roadside embankments, vacation lodges and park buildings: a living monument to the Works Progress Administration, the Depression-era jobs-creation programme of Franklin D. Roosevelt's New Deal.

41

For hardcore racers, there are local evening races during the summer on Tuesdays and Thursdays in far South Brooklyn. The course uses the old aerodrome of **Floyd Bennett Field**, former marshland that was reclaimed to create NYC's first commercial airport in the 1930s, before LaGuardia Airport on the north shore of Long Island took over. Just a mile or so from the sea and Rockaway Beach, the windy, exposed, crumbling concrete makes for gritty racing. An hour's ride from Lower Manhattan, it takes an intrepid *coureur* to brave the crazy rush-hour traffic all the way down Flatbush Ave (an old Indian trail before the Dutch settlers arrived). The reward is that, once there, you're communing with the very soul of New York City bike racing. George Hincapie used to crush it here as a junior.

For trackies, another obscure mecca is the **Kissena Velodrome** in Queens. The outdoor 402-m (440-yard) banked track, originally built in the 1960s by the city's master-builder Robert Moses, was until recently an advert for urban decay, with its frost-heaved cement and rusting ship-container equipment store. It is a strange paradox of a city that gave a name to a marquee track event, the Madison, that New York is without an indoor Olympic velodrome. The Madison acquired its name from the epic relay races of the late 19th and early 20th centuries that took place over days on the wooden boards of temporary indoor tracks erected in Madison Square Park (the original Madison Square Garden, adjacent to the glorious Flatiron Building on 5th Ave and 23rd St, and not to be confused with the 1960s brutalist monstrosity above Penn Station, home to basketball, ice hockey and stadium rock).

Recently improved, the Kissena Velodrome now has a smooth asphalt surface and a growing programme of events. If you're riding back into town from there, the natural route takes you through Corona Park, another Moses project replete with the weird, monumental relics of the 1964 World's Fair. The car, not the bike, was king in the city Moses built. His last great project, the Verrazano-Narrows Bridge between Brooklyn and Staten Island, which was the largest suspension bridge in the world when it opened in 1964, did not include a bike or pedestrian path (unlike most of other bridges in NYC). If you want to visit Staten Island, you can take your bike on the ferry, which leaves every 15 to 20 minutes from the South Ferry dock at Manhattan's southernmost tip. The views are magnificent – and it's free.

The only time you can ride the Verrazano Bridge today is if you take part in the **Five Boro Bike Tour**, when, as for the Marathon, the bridge is closed to traffic. It's a worthy event, for all the family, but expect heavy congestion and an awful lot of slow, weaving recreational riders. For the more ambitious and curious rider, a better bet by far is the annual **Bike the Boros** century ride, organized by the city's leading environmental transport organization, **Transportation Alternatives**: you don't get Staten Island, but you see far more of the other four boroughs.

To ride New York is to own it.

ESSENTIAL BIKE INFO

At first sight, the grid system of streets and avenues that dominates most of the city is intrinsically rational and makes navigation straightforward and intuitive. That is all true, but it doesn't reckon with New Yorkers themselves. For a European visitor, used to well-regulated traffic controls, reasonably uniform law enforcement and cultural norms of compliance by road users, the anarchic character of New York traffic may be a shock. In reality, it's no worse than many cities, and cycling is on the up here. But the key to being safe and enjoying your urban riding is being attuned to the unwritten rules of the road: the customs and culture of New York's road users. So here's what you need to know to survive and thrive.

RULES

Most road users in New York are notorious scofflaws, cyclists as well as drivers. Enforcement (see 'Police', below) is lax or random. So when it comes to offenses like texting while driving and excessive use of the horn, the law is more honoured in the breach than the observance.

As for the one-way bike lanes, they are treated as two-way highways – not just by cyclists, but also by skateboarders, pedestrians with earphones, food-cart proprietors, in-line skaters, motorized wheelchair users, and food-delivery guys. Compliance with red lights is so rare that pedestrians will spontaneously thank you for stopping instead of blowing through. Obeying the law is, of course, the higher path, but try not to be annoyed if your fine example is ignored by other bike-lane users; attempts at corrective action will only raise your blood pressure.

DRIVERS

New Yorkers are proverbially always in a hurry, and motorists are not used to finding bicycle riders on their roads. They generally regard cycling as a recreational activity, mostly for children before they grow up and become obese. America is not overtly a class society, but since a high proportion of people driving cars in the city have driven in from the suburbs, their attitudes have an edge of resentment: an adult on a bike is either a tourist who knows no better or, probably, a trust-funded WASP with a weekend place in the Hamptons. Neither deserves consideration, which is why cyclists in New York must simply expect as a matter of course that a car making a turn will cut across them with blithe disregard. Don't even bother to get indignant.

CABS

Despite Uber, yellow cabs are still ubiquitous. Taxi driving tends to be the employment of first resort for many new immigrants to the city. This contributes to the chaotic character of New York driving culture, because so many cab drivers originally learned to drive anywhere from Albania to Uzbekistan, and everywhere in between.

Some are cautious and, to their paying passengers, obtusely slow; others are lane-chopping maniacs. Odds are that at any given moment on any city block, you will find the full spectrum. Onto this anarchic driving culture is grafted a specific form of yellow-cab-crazy. Taxis answer only to the economic imperative of picking up and tipping out passengers. To do so, they will stop anywhere and block anything. They do not need to pull over to the side of the road, and generally won't.

Passengers aid and abet this impulsive behaviour, and will recklessly disembark from either side of a stationary cab, or any car, in the middle of the road. This is particularly crucial for cyclists to know, because it means that on New York's many one-way streets you can be 'doored' on either side of any line of stopped traffic.

POLICE

The NYPD may be known as New York's Finest, but they're also New York's most arbitrary. In general, they're not terribly interested in enforcing traffic laws – until they are. As a cyclist, you can run red lights all year round and never get a ticket. But the day after a cop will step off the curb, stop you and issue you with a ticket for around £160 ($200) or more (a cyclist can be fined for running a red at the same rate as a motorist). And if you can't show ID, you may find yourself 'summonsed' into the bargain.

The best advice is to show respect and act submissive. Your best hope is that the officer will not really want to bother with the paperwork, and you will get away with a reprimand. If, however, the precinct has decided on a ticketing blitz in a particular location, then it's best just to suck it up. If you live abroad and are visiting, you can almost certainly get away with ignoring the citation: Interpol will not come knocking.

ROADS

New York enjoys harsh winters, sporadic public spending and constant excavation by utilities. So road surfaces vary from carpet to moonscape; beware of potholes, ridges, even sinkholes. On the plus side, for aficionados of pavé, there are still some picturesque cobbled streets downtown in Tribeca and the West Village.

SECURITY

There's not as much bike parking as there should be, but plenty of other street furniture to use. Bike theft is a risk, but not an epidemic. A tatty town bike with a good lock is reasonably safe. Anything better and more valuable, though, should live with you in your apartment or in secure storage.

CITY BIKES AND BIKE HIRE

The **Citi Bike** scheme is a qualified success, and now operates in a large swathe of Manhattan, as well as parts of Brooklyn, Queens, even Jersey City. After initial troubles with financing and system software, it has proved enduring and popular. But it's relatively pricey ($12 for a day pass) for one-off users, and there are still problems with reliability and access at peak periods. The bikes are hefty clunkers, obviously.

In addition, there are private-hire businesses, catering mainly to tourists, along the Hudson River Path and in Central Park; but these offer utility bikes, and the rates are not great. More bike shops now are serving the higher end of the rental market with decent road bikes; but expect to pay accordingly. The nonprofit organization **Bike New York** is a useful resource for further information.

PUBLIC TRANSPORT

Mass transit in New York is not, historically, geared to making life easy for cyclists. You cannot, for instance, take a bike on **Amtrak** (the national rail service), unless it's broken down and bagged. Commuter rail services, like the **Metro-North Railroad** out of **Grand Central Terminal**, do generally allow bicycles, but there's no special provision for dedicated space and you may need a permit along with your ticket. Also, it can be a nightmare at rush-hour times. But these rail services are your best option for exploring rural rides within two hours of the city.

One peculiar boon to NYC cyclists is that bikes are allowed on the subway system. Again, you wouldn't even want to try it at peak times, but it's good to know about if it will save you from being soaked in a rainstorm on your way back from an evening out. Bikes are not allowed on buses, however. Full details can be found at the Department of Transportation site: nyc.gov.

AIR TRAVEL TO NYC

Most international carriers will treat a bike bag as check-in luggage, up to 23 kg (around 50 lbs), with no extra charge. But some American airlines, following the trend of domestic carriers, will now charge extra for outsize sports equipment, so check with your airline before departure.

Both of New York's international airports, **JFK** and **Newark,** have air trains that take you to the nearest transport hub. From Newark, the only option is to catch a train (**NJ Transit** or Amtrak) into **Penn Station** in midtown Manhattan; it's reasonably frequent and affordable. From JFK, you can take the A-train or E-train subway into New York; the E-train is a better choice (allow about 50 minutes) than the A-train (allow at least an hour). Quicker, but a bit more expensive, is taking the **Long Island Rail Road** in to Penn Station.

These are your best options if you're carrying a bike bag. A cab is far costlier and may not easily accommodate your luggage.

LINKS & ADDRESSES

79TH ST BOAT BASIN CAFE
W 79th St,
New York, NY 10024
boatbasincafe.com

AMERICAN MUSEUM OF NATURAL HISTORY
Central Park West and 79th St,
New York, NY 10024
amnh.org

APPLE SOHO
103 Prince St,
New York, NY 10012
apple.com/retail/soho

ATRIUM DUMBO
15 Main St,
Brooklyn, NY 11201
atriumdumbo.com

AUTOMATIC SLIM'S
733 Washington St,
New York, NY 10014
automaticslims.netwaiter.com

AZUCAR
334 S 4th St,
Brooklyn, NY 11211
facebook.com/azucaricecreamparlor

BAKED
359 Van Brunt St,
Brooklyn, NY 11231
bakednyc.com

BALTHAZAR
80 Spring St,
New York, NY 10012
balthazarny.com

BENNETT PARK
W 183rd St and
Fort Washington Ave,
New York, NY 10033
nycgovparks.org/parks/bennett-park

BKM CAFE & BOWL
200 Eastern Pkwy,
Brooklyn, NY 11238
brooklynmuseum.org/visit/hours_
admission/dining

BLUESTONE LANE
• 2 E 90th St,
  New York, NY 10128
• 55 Prospect St,
  Brooklyn, NY 11201
bluestonelaneny.com

BROOKLYN BOTANIC GARDEN
990 Washington Ave,
Brooklyn, NY 11225
bbg.org

BROOKLYN BRIDGE
New York, NY 10038
nyc.gov/html/dot/html/infrastructure/
brooklyn-bridge

BROOKLYN CRAB
24 Reed St,
Brooklyn, NY 11231
brooklyncrab.com

BROOKLYN FLEA
80 Pearl St,
Brooklyn, NY 11201
brooklynflea.com

BROOKLYN ICE CREAM FACTORY
1 Water St,
Brooklyn, NY 11201
brooklynicecreamfactory.com

BROOKLYN MUSEUM
200 Eastern Pkwy,
Brooklyn, NY 11238
brooklynmuseum.org

BROOKLYN NAVY YARD
63 Flushing Ave,
Brooklyn, NY 11205
brooklynnavyyard.org

BROOKLYN ROASTING COMPANY
240 Kent Ave,
Brooklyn, NY 11249
brooklynroasting.com

BUNBURY'S COFFEE SHOP
60 Piermont Ave,
Piermont, NY 10968
facebook.com/BunburysCoffee

CAFE BUUNNI
213 Pinehurst Ave,
New York, NY 10033
buunnicoffee.com

CAFE GRUMPY
383 7th Ave,
Brooklyn, NY 11215
cafegrumpy.com

CAFFÈ STORICO
170 Central Park West,
New York, NY 10024
nyhistory.org/dine/storico

CAT'S PAW
Central Park,
New York, NY 10024
centralpark.com/maps/locate/1085/
cats-paw

CBGB
315 Bowery, New York, NY 10003
cbgb.com

CHELSEA GALLERY DISTRICT
chelseagallerymap.com

CHURCH OF THE HEAVENLY REST
2 E 90th St,
New York, NY 10128
heavenlyrest.org

CITY RELIQUARY
370 Metropolitan Ave,
Brooklyn, NY 11211
cityreliquary.org

CITY WINERY
155 Varick St,
New York, NY 10013
citywinery.com

COUNTRY BOYS
568 4th Ave,
Brooklyn, NY 11215
countryboysfood.weebly.com

DEAN & DELUCA
560 Broadway,
New York, NY 10012
deandeluca.com

DOMINO SUGAR REFINERY
Kent Ave,
Brooklyn, NY 11211

DYCKMAN FARMHOUSE
4881 Broadway,
New York, NY 10034
dyckmanfarmhouse.org

EAR INN
326 Spring St,
New York, NY 10013
earinn.com

EL OLOMEGA
155 Bay St #1,
Brooklyn, NY 11231
elolomega.com

ENGINEER'S GATE
Central Park,
New York, NY 10024
centralpark.com/maps/locate/4137/
engineers-gate

FORT DEFIANCE
365 Van Brunt St,
Brooklyn, NY 11231
fortdefiancebrooklyn.com

FORT TRYON PARK
Riverside Dr to Broadway,
New York, NY 10040
nycgovparks.org/parks/fort-tryon-park

FORT WASHINGTON LIBRARY
535 W 179th St,
New York, NY 10033
nypl.org/locations/fort-washington

FRANKIES 457
457 Court St,
Brooklyn, NY 11231
frankiesspuntino.com

FREEMANS RESTAURANT
Freeman Alley,
New York, NY 10002
freemansrestaurant.com

GEORGE WASHINGTON BRIDGE
Fort Lee, NJ 07024
panynj.gov/bridges-tunnels/george-
washington-bridge

GIMME! COFFEE
228 Mott St,
New York, NY 10012
gimmecoffee.com

GORILLA COFFEE
97 5th Ave,
Brooklyn, NY 11217
gorillacoffee.com

GRAND ARMY PLAZA
Flatbush Ave,
Brooklyn, NY 11238
centralparknyc.org/things-to-see-
and-do/attractions/grand-army-plaza

GREENE SPACE
44 Charlton St,
New York, NY 10013
thegreenespace.org

GRIMALDI'S PIZZA
1 Front St, Brooklyn, NY 11201
grimaldis-pizza.com

GUGGENHEIM MUSEUM
1071 5th Ave,
New York, NY 10128
guggenheim.org

**GYPSY DONUT AND
ESPRESSO BAR**
18 N Franklin St,
Nyack, NY 10960
gypsydonut.com

HAMPTON CHUTNEY CO.
143 Grand St,
New York, NY 10013
hamptonchutney.com

**HEBREW TABERNACLE OF
WASHINGTON HEIGHTS**
551 Fort Washington Ave,
New York, NY 10033
hebrewtabernacle.org

HIGH LINE
91 Gansevoort St,
New York, NY 10014
thehighline.org

HOMETOWN BAR-B-QUE
454 Van Brunt St,
Brooklyn, NY 11231
hometownbarbque.com

**HOUSING WORKS
BOOKSTORE CAFE**
126 Crosby St,
New York, NY 10012
housingworksbookstore.org

**INTREPID SEA,
AIR & SPACE MUSEUM**
Pier 86, W 46th St and 12th Ave,
New York, NY 10036
intrepidmuseum.org

INWOOD HILL PARK
Dyckman St,
New York, NY 10452
nycgovparks.org/parks/
inwood-hill-park

INWOOD LIBRARY
4790 Broadway,
New York, NY 10034
nypl.org/locations/inwood

INWOOD LOCAL
4957 Broadway,
New York, NY 10034
inwoodlocalnyc.com

JEWISH MUSEUM
1109 5th Ave,
New York, NY 10128
thejewishmuseum.org

KNITTING FACTORY
361 Metropolitan Ave,
Brooklyn, NY 11211
bk.knittingfactory.com

LA CIGOGNE
213–215 Union St,
Brooklyn, NY 11231
lacigognenyc.com

LA COLOMBE
154 Prince St,
New York, NY 10012
lacolombe.com

LA GAMELLE
241 Bowery,
New York, NY 10002
lagamellenyc.com

LA MARINA
348 Dyckman St,
New York, NY 10034
lamarinanyc.com

LE CHÉILE
839 W 181st St,
New York, NY 10033
lecheilenyc.com

LE PAIN QUOTIDIEN
2 W 69th St,
New York, NY 10023
lepainquotidien.com/store/central-
park-mineral-springs

LOBSTER POUND
284 Van Brunt St,
Brooklyn, NY 11231
redhooklobster.com

LOEB BOATHOUSE
E 72nd St,
New York, NY 10021
thecentralparkboathouse.com

LORELEY BEER GARDEN
7 Rivington St,
New York, NY 10002
loreleynyc.com

LUCKY DOG
303 Bedford Ave,
Brooklyn, NY 11211
facebook.com/luckydogbrooklyn

MAMASUSHI
237 Dyckman St,
New York, NY 10040
mamasushi.com

MANHATTAN BRIDGE
New York, NY 11201
nyc.gov/html/dot/html/infrastructure/
manhattan-bridge

**MANHATTAN COMMUNITY
BOATHOUSE**
Hudson River Greenway,
New York, NY 10019
manhattancommunityboathouse.org

MCNALLY JACKSON
52 Prince St,
New York, NY 10012
mcnallyjackson.com

MERCURY LOUNGE
217 E Houston St,
New York, NY 10002
mercuryloungenyc.com

**METROPOLITAN MUSEUM
OF ART + MET ROOF GARDEN
CAFE AND MARTINI BAR**
1000 5th Ave,
New York, NY 10028
metmuseum.org

MOMA DESIGN STORE
81 Spring St A,
New York, NY 10012
store.moma.org

**MUSEUM OF THE
CITY OF NEW YORK**
1220 5th Ave,
New York, NY 10029
mcny.org

NEUE GALERIE
1048 5th Ave,
New York, NY 10028
neuegalerie.org

NEW MUSEUM
235 Bowery,
New York, NY 10002
newmuseum.org

NEW-YORK HISTORICAL SOCIETY
170 Central Park West,
New York, NY 10024
nyhistory.org

NITEHAWK CINEMA
136 Metropolitan Ave,
Brooklyn, NY 11249
nitehawkcinema.com

PAPASITO
223 Dyckman St,
New York, NY 10034
papasito.nyc

OTHER HALF BREWING CO.
195 Centre St,
Brooklyn, NY 11231
otherhalfbrewing.com

PARK WEST CAFE AND DELI
477 Central Park West,
New York, NY 10025
parkwestcafeanddeli.com

PRIME MEATS
465 Court St,
Brooklyn, NY 11231
frankspm.com

RED HOOK BAIT & TACKLE
320 Van Brunt St,
Brooklyn, NY 11231
redhookbaitandtackle.com

RED HOOK FOOD VENDORS
Red Hook Recreation Fields,
160 Bay St, Brooklyn, NY 11231
redhookfoodvendors.com

RIVERSIDE PARK
New York, NY 10025
nycgovparks.org/parks/riverside-park

RUNCIBLE SPOON BAKERY
7 N Broadway,
Nyack, NY 10960
facebook.com/RuncibleSpoonBakery

RUSS & DAUGHTERS
127 Orchard St,
New York, NY 10002
russanddaughterscafe.com

RYE
247 S 1st St,
Brooklyn, NY 11211
ryerestaurant.com

ST ANN'S WAREHOUSE
45 Water St,
Brooklyn, NY 11201
stannswarehouse.org

ST MARY'S STAR OF THE SEA
467 Court St,
Brooklyn, NY 11231
stmarystarbrooklyn.com

ST LUKE IN THE FIELDS
487 Hudson St,
New York, NY 10014
stlukeinthefields.org

ST PATRICK'S OLD CATHEDRAL
45 Prince St,
New York, NY 10012
oldcathedral.org

SCOTTADITO
788a Union St,
Brooklyn, NY 11215
scottadito.com

SMORGASBURG
90 Kent Ave, Brooklyn, NY 11211
smorgasburg.com

SOHO ROOM
203 Spring St, #C,
New York, NY 10012
sohoroomnyc.com

STATE LINE LOOKOUT
Palisades Interstate Pkwy,
Alpine, NJ 07620
njpalisades.org/stateline

STRAWBERRY FIELDS
Central Park West at W 72nd St,
New York, NY 10023
centralparknyc.org/things-to-see-
and-do/attractions/strawberry-fields

TAVERN ON THE GREEN
Central Park West and 67th St,
New York, NY 10023
tavernonthegreen.com

TENEMENT MUSEUM
103 Orchard St,
New York, NY 10002
tenement.org

THE CLOISTERS
99 Margaret Corbin Dr,
New York, NY 10040
metmuseum.org

THE DAKOTA
1 W 72nd St,
New York, NY 10023

THE ELDORADO
300 Central Park West,
New York, NY 10024

THE LAKE
Central Park,
New York, NY 10024
centralparknyc.org/things-to-see-
and-do/attractions/boating

THE SAN REMO
145 Central Park West,
New York, NY 10023

THE PARK VIEW
219 Dyckman St,
New York, NY 10034
theparkviewcafe.com

THE SPOTTED PIG
314 W 11th St,
New York, NY 10014
thespottedpig.com

TOM & JERRY'S
288 Elizabeth St,
New York, NY 10012
facebook.com/TomJerry.288

TRIE CAFE
99 Margaret Corbin Dr,
New York, NY 10040
metmuseum.org

TRYON PUBLIC HOUSE
4740 Broadway,
New York, NY 10040
tryonpublichouse.com

VAN CORTLANDT PARK
Broadway and
Van Cortlandt Park S,
Bronx, NY 10462
nycgovparks.org/parks/
VanCortlandtPark

VESUVIO BAKERY
160 Prince St,
New York, NY 10012

VESUVIO PLAYGROUND
Thompson St,
New York, NY 10012
nycgovparks.org/parks/
vesuvio-playground

VINEGAR HILL HOUSE
72 Hudson Ave,
Brooklyn, NY 11201
vinegarhillhouse.com

WATCHTOWER
25 Columbia Heights,
Brooklyn, NY 11201
jw.org

WHITE HORSE TAVERN
567 Hudson St,
New York, NY 10014
facebook.com/
Whitehorsetavern1880nyc

**WHITNEY MUSEUM OF
AMERICAN ART**
99 Gansevoort St,
New York, NY 10014
whitney.org

WILLIAMSBURG BRIDGE
New York, NY 11104
nyc.gov/html/dot/html/infrastructure/
williamsburg-bridge

WOLLMAN RINK
830 5th Ave,
New York, NY 10065
wollmanskatingrink.com

**BIKE SHOPS, CLUBS,
RACES AND VENUES**

BICYCLE HABITAT
250 Lafayette St,
New York, NY 10012
bicyclehabitat.com

BIKE NEW YORK
bike.nyc

BIKEREG
bikereg.com

BIKE THE BOROS
bike.nyc

**CENTURY ROAD CLUB
ASSOCIATION**
crca.net

CITI BIKE
citibikenyc.com

FIVE BORO BIKE TOUR
bike.nyc

FLOYD BENNETT FIELD
1 Floyd Bennett Fld,
Brooklyn, NY 11234
nyharborparks.org/visit/flbe

GRAN FONDO
gfny.com

HUDSON RIVER PARK BIKEWAY
hudsonriverpark.org/explore-the-park/
activities/bicycling

KISSENA VELODROME
Flushing, NY 11355
kissenavelodrome.info

**RAPHA CLUBHOUSE
& CYCLING CLUB**
159 Prince St,
New York, NY 10012
rapha.cc

**TRANSPORTATION
ALTERNATIVES**
111 John St, Suite 260,
New York, NY 10038
transalt.org

TREAD BIKE SHOP
250 Dyckman St,
New York, NY 10034
treadbikeshop.com

OTHER USEFUL SITES

AMTRAK
amtrak.com

GRAND CENTRAL TERMINAL
89 E 42nd St,
New York, NY 10017
grandcentralterminal.com

**JOHN F. KENNEDY
INTERNATIONAL AIRPORT**
Queens, NY 11430
panynj.gov/airports/jfk

LONG ISLAND RAIL ROAD
mta.info/lirr

METRO-NORTH RAILROAD
mta.info/mnr

**NEWARK LIBERTY
INTERNATIONAL AIRPORT**
3 Brewster Rd,
Newark, NJ 07114
panynj.gov/airports/newark-liberty

NJ TRANSIT
njtransit.com

PENN STATION
8th Ave and W 31st St,
New York, NY 10001

NOTES

Rapha, established in London, has always been a champion of city cycling – from testing our first prototype jackets on the backs of bike couriers, to a whole range of products designed specifically for the demands of daily life on the bike. As well as an online emporium of products, films, photography and stories, Rapha has a growing network of Clubhouses, locations around the globe where cyclists can enjoy live racing, food, drink and the latest products.

Rapha.